LUTHERAN

VOICES

Will I Sing Again?
Listening for the Melody of Grace in the Silence of Illness and Loss

John McCullough Bade

Augsburg Fortress
Minneapolis

WILL I SING AGAIN?
Listening for the Melody of Grace in the Silence of Illness and Loss

Direct Scripture quotations are from New Revised Standard Version Bible, copyright © 1989 Division of Christian Education of the National Council of the Churches of Christ in the United States of America. Used by permission.

Musical definitions, other than for "Program Notes" are from The American Heritage, Dictionary of the English Language, Fourth Edition, copyright © 2000 by Houghton Mifflin Company.

Editor: Susan R. Niemi

Cover Design: Koechel Peterson and Associates, Inc., Minneapolis, MN
                www.koechelpeterson.com

Cover photo: Koechel Peterson and Associates, Inc.

ISBN 0-8066-4998-4

The paper used in this publication meets the minimum requirements of American National Standard for Information Sciences—Permanence of Paper for Printed Library Materials, ANSI Z329.48-1984.

Manufactured in the U.S.A.

07   06   05   04   03   1   2   3   4   5   6   7   8   9   10

The Poet—Troubadour of the Melodies of Grace

It is foolish to think of such as this;
>   my phrases pale in the brilliant light of others' splendid verse,
>   bleached of color when spoken
>   with hushed tones beside their wondrous words.

And yet, we see life through similar eyes—
>   intense, plum-ripe,
>   lees on the vine,
>   all-at-once wondrous and tragic,
>   unfathomable in its ecstasy,
>   bottomless in its sorrow.

Dramatic, to be sure.
"Exaggerated," some might say.

But no.

To know the depths of despair
>   and the heights of joy . . .
To feel the brush of the ocean wind
>   combing out the tangled web of frantic living . . .
To taste the salt of frothing waters
>   preserving the sustenance of what was about to spoil . . .
To see the damp, dripping blanket of darkness lifted,
>   even for just a moment of starlit, shining clarity . . .
To savor the fullness of union
>   with One who is fulfillment, wholeness, peace . . .
What words can truly reflect such as this?

So, sing, we must;
>   no matter how softly—
>   of darkness, of light,
>   of love, of life,
>   of God.
Sing we must.

Contents

Foreword

In a 1997 letter of resignation to his congregation, Rev. John Bade wrote, "I have struggled mightily with this decision and its timing. . . . I do not plan to just sit at home with nothing to do. I have several aspirations—writing and extended study—to which I hope to devote significant time." This time devoted to writing has indeed been well spent, for he has masterfully created a powerful work through poetry and the metaphor of song that both poignantly describes his ongoing struggle with a chronic, increasingly debilitating illness, the choices he—and often we—all have, and the ultimate epiphany that through God's love, we can yet—become! Although the writer quickly engages the reader in his intimately personal experience, he does not become maudlin, but rather challenges us to insight into our own personal growth in faith.

The poem, "I May Be," brings consolation and the promise of hope. We learn "the curse becomes the blessing in the powerful, creative hands of God." He reaffirms the "cantus firmus"– the constant sound of God's voice reminding us that God gives us his Word and the strength and courage to "dare to choose life." "We can choose to keep listening for the melodies of grace . . . and to try to keep singing!" "It is the power of God found in weakness—the power of God to sing in the silence and pain of the world."

As communities of faith, the poem "Tapestry," reaffirms how "God weaves us together . . . And our lives are all the richer and more beautiful because of the tapestry of which we are a part." Many readers will especially resonate to the "Hymn to the Apothecary," and the reflection of Christ as the "wounded Healer." Rev. John Bade's work, however, speaks to us all, and testifies that ministry transcends the bounds of physical limitation; again confirming what care providers have long known, that those cared for often minister to us profoundly, in ways far beyond the care we may provide.

Thanks be to God!
Cynthia Prestholdt, Ph.D., R.N.
Baton Rouge, Louisiana

Overture

"You have Parkinson's disease."

I was thirty-one years old on that bright October afternoon in 1989
when I first heard these words of the neurologist. I was serving a
church in Austin, Texas—just beginning my ministry as an ordained
pastor. Life was filled with music and promise. I was surrounded by
a community of faith and by people who supported and loved me.
All seemed in harmony and right with the world.

"You have Parkinson's disease."

I heard the words, yet I didn't hear them at all. A deep silence
covered the remainder of my doctor's appointment that day. Just
a few hours earlier, I had visited an elderly parishioner who was
afflicted with Parkinson's, and I knew and saw firsthand the difficult
road he was walking. And now, that journey was to be mine as well.

"You have Parkinson's disease."

Over the years since that diagnosis, I have experienced the wide-
ranging emotions that accompany chronic illness and loss. The
voices in my life—of doubt and faith, frustration and contentment,
anger and joy, despair and hope—have all, at one time or another,
spoken within me. Undergirding their sounds has been the
promise of God. At times, that promise has seemed silenced—
buried by the weight and demands that illness and loss bring. And
at other times, God's presence and promise have been heard loudly
and clearly.

Often, those who experience loss (as well as their caregivers) are so consumed by the challenges of daily living that they can neither perceive nor scarcely articulate the myriad sounds of faith and hope, doubt and despair in their lives. The tendency for many is to withdraw into the silence, where the melodies of grace are difficult to hear.

This book is an attempt to listen to the music of life. The title—*Will I Sing Again?*—reflects both the silence of loss and the hope-filled promise of a melody yet to come. The voice heard in this book is of one living with a chronic illness, but I believe the verses resonate for anyone who has faced the pain of illness, the despair of broken relationships, the sorrow of loss.

Through meditations, reflections, poetry, and story you are invited to eavesdrop on the melody of my life—the sounds of silence as well as the melodies of grace. Each chapter is introduced by a melody of the Bible—a portion of a psalm—as well as a reflection from another author. And each includes an autobiographical note to mark the point in time in which the chapter is placed—in musical terms, a "measure marker" of the placement of the movement. At the end of each chapter, you are encouraged to listen to your own melodies through a series of questions and reflections.

I hope that the melodies of my life might give voice to your life's song—both the harmonies and the dissonance, the silence and the sounds. And I pray that you might in some way hear in the music of your life the melody of God's presence and grace that brings hope, promise, peace, and forgiveness.

John McCullough Bade

The First Movement

∽

From Melody to Silence

1

Harmony

A combination of sounds considered pleasing to the ear

Praise the Lord! How good it is to sing praises to our God; for (God) is gracious, and a song of praise is fitting.

 ▪ *Psalm 147:1*

The virtuosity (or special calling) of a person . . . is the melody of that person's life.

 ▪ *Friedrich Schleiermacher*

Friedrich Schleiermacher, *On Religion: Addresses in Response to Its Cultured Critics*, John Knox Press, 1969. Quoted in Jaroslav Pelikan's book *The Melody of Theology: A Philosophical Dictionary*, copyright 1988 Harvard University Press, Cambridge, MA., page v of the preface.

The melody of my life

I began my ordained ministry three years prior to the initial diagnosis of Parkinson's disease. I had enjoyed the challenges of seminary and was ready to serve Christ as a pastor in the church. I was called to a congregation in the growing city of Austin, Texas.

I saw God as a God of covenants—One who enters into relationship with us. My ministry was hope-filled and shaped around the sure promises of God.

Life, too, seemed full of hope and promise. I embraced the challenges of these early years of ordained ministry with enthusiasm and joy. I was healthy and full of energy. It was easy to sing praises to God. Life seemed to be just beginning.

Once, Upon a Time

Once, upon a time,
  Life was filled with music;
    Hope sang loud and strong.
  Possibilities stretched endless;
    Promise shone as dawn.
Once, upon a time,
  Paths were clear and easy;
    Burdens few and light.
  Cares were free, forgotten;
    Worries out of sight.
Once, upon a time,
  Faith was never questioned;
    Covenants were sure.
  Loss was lost, unmeasured;
    Illness knew a cure.

Once, upon a time,
  Melodies came easy;
    Notes rang out in time.
  Music flowed in sequence;
    Words and lyrics rhymed.
Once, upon a time,
  God was near, omniscient—
    Spirit, Comfort, Guide.
  Praise broke sorrow's silence;
    Death and grief had died.

Once, upon a time,
>> I scarce could keep from singing
>>>> Life's sweet melody.
>> Joy burst clouds of sadness;
>>>> No strife, serenity.

Once,
>> Once, upon a time.

A New Creation

The clouds hung high over the trees,
        their thin cover a transparent mask
                filtering the brightness of the full moon.

Reflections danced a shadowy image on the still waters.

In the distance,
        the gurgling of a waterfall faintly joined
                the monotonous song of the creatures of the night—
                        frogs, crickets, owls.

All was masked, veiled—
        seen but not seen,
        heard but not understood,
        reflected, but not fully experienced.

And then it happened.

High above the stilled treetops,
        far from our earthbound path,
        blowing from the very throne of heaven,
                the Spirit/Wind blew the clouds aside.

The moon shone bright and full,
        unencumbered by the veil of the past,
        radiantly beaming in its purity and glory.
And with the unveiling,
        the water reflected full and clear
                the beauty of God's creation.
All the stars paled in its light.

Suddenly, the whole world became alive—
    a symphony of sound—
    unfiltered, unrestrained,
    a melody of sheer delight and wonderment,
       of awe and unbridled joy.

For one shining moment,
    Life . . . and love
    Light . . . and beauty
       were seen and heard and experienced
         with such intensity and clarity
          such acceptance and celebration and passion
        that I was left breathless, speechless, awestruck.

And a voice was heard to say,
    "Let it be so,"
       and it was so;
    and behold,
       it was very, very good.

Listening to your melodies

- Reflect on times of great hope and celebration in your life.
- Describe a time when you felt particularly alive, strong, or hope-filled. Is that time limited only to times of health and wholeness?
- What brings you joy today?
- How do illness and loss "color" the way you view and experience the world?
- How might you experience more moments of hope and celebration within your life?

2

Dissonance

A harsh, disagreeable combination of sounds; discord

*A combination of tones contextually considered to
suggest unrelieved tension and require resolution*

Out of the depths I cry to you, O Lord. Lord, hear my voice!
   Psalm 130:1–2

*We are, God knows, a people who walk in darkness . . . Darkness fills
the skies over our own cities no less than over the cities of our enemies.
And in our single lives, we know much about darkness, too. If we are
people who pray, darkness is apt to be a lot of what our prayers are
about. If we are people who do not pray, it is apt to be darkness in one
form or another that has stopped our mouths.*

   Frederich Buechner

Frederich Buechner, *The Hungering Dark*, Harper and Row, 1969, p. 50.

The melody of my life

It was a subtle beginning—a slight tremor in my right hand that wouldn't go away. I remember sitting on the couch one evening and not being able to keep my right hand from shaking. I had been keeping a busy schedule, so I dismissed the shaking as a symptom of fatigue that would cease once I got some rest.

But it didn't go away. Finally, I made an appointment to see a doctor. I hadn't been ill often enough to even need a family doctor before. I was referred to a neurologist who made the initial diagnosis. The neurologist then referred me to a specialist in movement disorders who confirmed the news—I had Parkinson's disease.

The struggle with chronic illness and lingering grief is a constant battle. The illness and its effects shouted loudly in my life; and in response, I withdrew into a certain silence. It demanded my energies and sapped me of hope and strength. In time, it required a major life change—I resigned my call as parish pastor and went on permanent disability. The illness seemed to have drowned out the sound of God's presence and promise.

The Day the Poetry Died

Some things are marked in their passing—
>   the death of a loved one
>   the birth of a child
>   love's first kiss.

And some things go away so gradually
>   that their passing goes almost unnoticed—
>   fallen leaves of autumn tumbling down,
>   down, down
>   until suddenly the great oak tree is bare.

I really don't remember what day it was,
>   the day the poetry died.

Was it Spring,
>   when new growth was pushing up through the soil,
>   and I had no words to celebrate?

Was it Fall,
>   when the kaleidoscope of colors dazzled others,
>   and all I saw were brown, dead leaves?

Was it Summer,
>   when the warmth of creation allowed for new growth,
>   and all I could see was the afternoon haze,
>   and all I felt was the scorching heat?

Or was it Winter,
>   when ice and snow created winter wonderlands,
>   and all I could see was treacherous terrain,
>   and all I felt was the numbing cold?

What day was it,
>> the day the poetry died?

Yes, it was Winter . . .
>> Winter for too long,
>>> the pen frozen,
>>> the wellspring blocked with ice,
>>> the road full of salt that burned in the wounds.

The exact date I don't remember,
>> that winter day the poetry died.

I was walking the perilous slippery path,
>> covered with ice and snow,
>> when suddenly I looked up and saw the empty trees,
>>> the branches bare
>>> the fruit all gone
>>> barely able to give shelter and shade to others.

Oh, how I have yearned,
>> though I could not give the yearning a voice,
>>> for the words to come again
>>> for the warmth of Spring
>>> for the clear waters of melted snow
>>>> to rush forth and give voice
>>>>> to the grief and loss felt
>>>>>> the day the poetry died.

Aches and Pains

I sit before the computer screen,
>the left hand bouncing on and off the keyboard,
>the right stiffly, slowly moving from key to key.

Words become a confusing array of letters
>as one key is inadvertently hit,
>another accidentally held down—
>>Ls and Ss littering the written landscape.

My head bounces slightly from side to side;
>my neck muscles taut from holding it still.

My calf muscles are as strings on a guitar—
>tight, pulling from end to end,
>playing a nervous, painful, weary melody.

Toes on one foot curl down,
>seeking release from an unseen force
>>that demands their movement,
>>>even when none is needed or welcomed.
To purposely move with intention
>calls forth intense concentration,
>a deliberate willing of the mind to make the body move;
And to stop the unwelcome tremors
>takes more energy than I have to give.

Stress . . . Anxiety . . . Weariness . . .
>An all-too-busy schedule . . .
Are these aches and pains the result of situations such as these,
>or is this a glimpse of my future relationship
>>with this unwelcome guest?

I have learned how to conceal all these struggles,
       hoping that if I never speak them,
              they have no power over me.

But the trembling arm,
       the lethargic leg,
       the bone-tired weariness
       the multiple medications
              stand as daily reminders
                     of the presence of this mysterious illness.

In some ways, my concealment—which was my strength—
              now has come to haunt me.

For I hid the struggle so capably
       that many might not believe
              the depth and intensity of the adversity.

"The spirit is willing,
       but the flesh is weak."

Is the source of my aches and pain this night
       the intruding disease,
or is it another deeper, distant, unspoken pain?

No answer will be found . . .
Not tonight . . . not tonight.

And so, with a sigh too deep for words,
       I slowly, deliberately finish the phrase.
I shut down . . . and wait for the promise
       of the morning's light.

Exile

By the rivers . . . there we sat down and there we wept when we remembered Zion. On the willows there we hung up our harps. For there our captors asked us for songs, and our tormentors asked for mirth, saying, "Sing us one of the songs of Zion!" How could we sing the Lord's song in a foreign land?

    Psalm 137

They say it is the same moon that shines at night . . .
The same stars light the dark sky. I suppose it might
be the same as what I used to see
before my life changed
       and I was no longer free
           to be the me I thought You intended me to be.

They say the same sun rises o'er the eastern hills,
the same wind blows across the water and fills
the same sails with power to glide and go
across the same rough seas. So they say. But I don't know
       who I am anymore or where I can be truly free
           to be the me I thought You intended me to be.

They say the same song can be sung anywhere;
after all, it's just a song, so why should they care
if I sing it because they demand my mirth
as if I had a choice in death or in birth
       or a choice in whether I sing truly free
           as the me I thought You intended me to be.

They say, "Home is where the heart is,"
a place of peace and calm,
a place where fears are cast away,
      a place where wounds find balm.
If that be so, this is no home, this place of misery . . .
      this place where I can never be
            the me I thought You wanted me to be.

Why always, "No"? Why never, "Yes"?
Why never, "Friend"? Why always, "Guest"?
Why is it, "They"? Why never, "We"?
Why always, "Do"? Why never, "Be"?
      Will my longing eyes ever see
            the me I thought You intended me to be?

The Boxer

Eyes bloodshot and swollen,
  almost shut from pain and sheer exhaustion.
Face puffy,
  black circles surrounding, enveloping,
   entrapping what little energy remains in this contorted face.
Legs unsteady,
  wobbling to keep balance . . .
Arms forcibly raised,
  lead weight pulling them down . . . down . . . down.

Wearily, the boxer steps into the ring
  to fight yet another round—
   a strange, never-ending match.
    Disease, disability, and loss.

Each has its own weapons . . .
Each has its own rules of engagement . . .
Each calls forth—demands—
  the strength of this weary, battered shell of a man.

The sound of the bell simultaneously signifies the end of one round
  and the beginning of another.
No time for rest . . .
  No corner to claim as his own;
The only reprieve, the time it takes to travel
  from one ring to another.

Someday, there will be a final bell
  announcing that the battles are done.
But tonight,
  Tonight the fight goes on.

The bell sounds,
>
> and the boxer slowly, painfully climbs through the ropes
>> as the struggle begins again.

Weary, drained, spent,
the boxer drops his arms to his side.

Dare he let his guard down,
> allowing his weariness to expose his vulnerability?
Or will even this one action
> be the one opening needed to deliver the blow
>> that plunges him to the canvas?

The tiredness of the hour
> weighs heavy on him,
>> tempting him to just give up.

But from somewhere deep within,
> this weary, wounded warrior finds a morsel of remaining strength,
>> and slowly, deliberately,
> his trembling, stone-heavy arms are lifted.
And once more, at least for one more round,
> the guard is in place.

The bell sounds the end of the round,
> and the boxer stumbles out of the ring,
>> bent, bloodied, and bowed,
> his wounds opened yet again.
But still standing . . .
> still standing, he waits to combat the next demon
>> that he faces alone
>>> this dark, lonely night of battle.

Weeds

It begins innocently enough.
A few errant weeds,
      unnoticed, scarcely seen by passersby—
      a few blades of grass stretching out
            beyond the curbed, paved boundary
              of health and well-being.

From whence they were seeded, no one knows.

With stealth and invasion
      they find soil and take root;
their stems push through fertile soil until at last
      they find the light of day.
Slowly, deliberately, incessantly,
      they spread . . . and are noticed by others.

As diligently as the tenant fights their invasion
      and attempts to conceal their presence and pull them out,
      even more so do they grow.

If life be a garden,
      then this illness is its weed—
            Pervasive, invasive, unwelcome, unwanted.

Will the gardener discover the remedy
before being overtaken by this evil guest?

Or will a way be found
      to cultivate and harness its unkept vine,
            so that fruit and flower can be harvested
              from what is known now as a weed?

Silence
(Based on the story of Elijah in 1 Kings 19)

Deep within me is heard
  the sounds of a silent scream—
    deafening in its lack of decibels,
    shattering the rhythms and familiar harmonies
     with its terrible void.

How does one hear such emptiness?
How does one give voice
  to such a voiceless sound?

This scream
  is seen and felt as well as heard.

It is seen in the volume of tears
  flowing from a well of wounds,
    its depth fathomless and unnamed—
     uncharted waters never entered or explored.

It is felt in the numbness
  spreading like a freezing cold
    stiffening all movement
    and halting all growth.

It is heard in the silence—
  the guttural moan
    rising from deep within—
     a moan of such intensity and unspeakable pain
      that nothing else can be expressed . . .

(continued)

Nothing . . .
          no words . . .
                    no sounds . . .
          No feelings . . .
                    only the faint whispering
                              of this deafening, silent scream.

What words can describe this deafening darkness?
What language can capture
          the depth of the wound,
          the darkness of the night,
          the intensity of this soundlessness?

I seek refuge from its noiseless sounds
          in the dark bowels of the desert cave,
                    feeling the scorching heat of the day
                              and the chilling cold of the night.
I am afraid . . .

For it feels like
          I . . .
                    even I alone,
                    am left,
          and they are seeking my life, to take it away.

The forces against me are myriad,
          and their voices are loud.
In the din of their sounds,
          it's hard to hear the sound of the silent scream.

I seek the presence of God
          in this deafening, noiseless cave.

The great wind blows,
>> so strong in its fury that boulders long-standing
>>> are shattered into pieces . . .
>>>> . . . but the Lord is not in the wind.

The land trembles and quakes;
>> familiar terrain is shaken
>>> and caste aside in its force . . .
>>>> . . . but the Lord is not in the quake.

And after the quake,
>> a raging fire burns up the scattered refuse
>>> of lost opportunities and unspoken dreams . . .
>>>> . . . but the Lord is not in the fire.

Exhausted . . .
>> I sit at the mouth of the cave—
>>> the boulder, which had blocked its entrance,
>>>> now broken into pieces . . .
>>> the familiar landscape of my existence
>>>> shattered . . .
>>> a dull burning fire smoldering within me,
>>>> its billowing smoke hanging over me like a pall . . .

And I feel from deep within
>> the sounds of sheer silence,
>> the voice of a silent scream.

In my weariness I wonder:
>> Could this be the voice of God?

Midnight

The siren screams out the warning—
      there is someone wounded, hurt,
          in sorrow, dying inside.

I hear its shrill sound as it goes past the window
      in the dark of the midnight hour.

Someone is grieving . . .
      someone is in pain.

I listen, and I wonder:
      Is there someone there to hear the cries
         of the one in pain in this midnight hour?

I am so weary . . .
      weary of the struggle
      weary of the tears
      weary from the day
      weary of fighting to be heard
         by doctors and technicians . . .
         by those who think they understand
            but who never ask and who never listen . . .
      weary of this journey that I have no choice but to travel.

I am asked to name the sorrow,
      to speak the anguish.

But I can't . . .

I, so skilled at crafting words
>>> and painting images on the printed page . . .
>> I don't have the words to speak.

The sorrow is too deep, too elemental,
>> too buried under the layers of pain and loss,
>>> of wanting to be heard but never knowing what to say,
>>> of wanting to pray but never finding the words,
>>> of experiencing the deep sadness
>>>>> of grief unnamed and sorrow unspoken,
>> that I have no words to say.

"The Spirit intercedes
>> in sighs too deep for words," Paul wrote.

And so I pray this night:
O Holy Spirit,
>> Speak the words I cannot speak.
>> Shed the tears I have no more energy to cry.
>> Intercede for me to the throne of God.
>> Carry my grief, my loss, my pain, my need
>>> to the very heart of Christ.
>> For I am spent, and I have no energy left
>>> to find the words.

>> And be with those in the darkness
>>> for whom the siren screams.
>> May they, too, be blest
>>> with Someone to hold them
>>>>> and Someone to speak their name in prayer
>>>>> in the pain of their midnight hour.

Rain Clouds

Outside, the rain begins to fall ...
     yet again ... yet again the clouds do come.

In another place and time,
     this rain brings life and energy,
        cleansing and growth;
     but today, it is a burden—
        too much to bear,
        drowning the very life it was created to nourish.

These rain clouds know what it is
     to shoulder an uninvited force,
     to bear the weight of their surroundings,
     to move with lethargy from one place to another.

They know the struggle to remain aloft
     as the heat of the day builds and builds
        until it is too much—
           too much to support
           too much to endure.

They know they must bear what must be borne;
     and so do I.

These trembling, lethargic limbs,
     this inner struggle ...
        all weigh heavily on my clouded existence.

I know I do not have opportunity to choose
    the path of the light, airy cloud
        with no burden to carry,
        no rain to release,
        no tears to fall.

And yet, there is a choice before me.

I can choose to shape my life
    so that the weight of the world
    might become a catalyst for new growth
        rather than a burden
        that drowns and disfigures me into something I am not.

And so, I hear the question of the rain clouds:

Do I allow the weight of the demands
        and the heat and weariness of the day
        to build up upon and within me
            until I am poured out,
            emptied,
                with nothing left to give,
                a faint, foggy mist of who and what I am?

Or dare I trust in the winds of the Spirit
    to move and guide me to shapes unknown?

The answer I choose
    may very well determine whether at the end of the day
        I am completely spent, invisible,
            long-evaporated in the afternoon sun;

(continued)

Or whether, as the evening comes,
> I am part of a beautiful sunset,
>> a signature work of the Master painter,
>>> reflecting the soft, beautiful colors
>>> of a day cherished,
>>>> a day celebrated and enjoyed,
>>>> a day well-lived.

Listening to your melodies

- What emotions do you experience when there is news of loss and illness?
- The author writes of illness as a weed. What are the weeds in your life?
- How would you describe your losses?
- Why do you think there is a tendency to withdraw in times of illness and loss? In what ways is God's presence felt?
- In what ways is "God-forsaken-ness" felt and expressed?
- How have you experienced silence in your life? Has it been a blessing or a curse?
- What do you do when weariness sets in?
- Where is God in your life's struggle?

The Second Movement

∾

From Silence to Song

3

The Cantus Firmus

The foundational melody used as the basis for a composition

Where can I go from your spirit? . . . If I say, "Surely the darkness shall cover me, and the light around me become night," even the darkness is not dark to you; the night is as bright as the day.

    Psalm 139: 7, 11

Even though I walk through the darkest valley, I fear no evil; for you are with me; your rod and your staff—they comfort me.

    Psalm 23: 4

Theological reflection is reflecting on the painful and joyful realities of every day with the mind of Jesus and hereby raising human consciousness to the knowledge of God's gentle guidance. This is a hard discipline, since God's presence is often a hidden presence, a presence that needs to be discovered. The loud, boisterous noises of the world make us deaf to the soft, gentle, and loving voice of God.

    Henri J. M. Nouwen*

---

*Henri J. M. Nouwen, *In the Name of Jesus: Reflections on Christian Leadership,* Crossroad Publishing Co, New York, 1999, pp. 68-69.

The melody of my life

I found myself dealing with the illness and its implications in a variety of ways. At times, I made deliberate changes to accommodate the growing physical limitations I experienced. Most of the time, I pushed myself to keep doing what I had always done, even though it took more and more energy to do so. Staying busy, even after my resignation from the full-time pastorate, kept me from facing the spiritual silence I was experiencing.

But slowly, over time, I have begun to hear God's voice in the midst of my suffering. Although I believe the voice is a constant sound—a cantus firmus—there are times when I find it difficult to hear it. But I trust God's voice is there.

Lost and Found

"Lost and Found!"
        "Find what you're missing here!"

The voice was but a whisper—
        scarcely audible over the din of rushing traffic
            and ringing phones,
       its sound unclear in the murky noises
            of blaring music and demands calling my name.

"Lost and Found!"

I hurried on . . .
       just another sound to add to the cacophonic harmony
           of a melody too full of notes.
       Just another sound . . .

For so long, I had been able to ignore its distant call.
For so long, I was sure I knew the phrasing.
For so long, the melody of my daily existence
       had been loud enough to drown out
           this soft voice quietly singing,
             "Lost and Found! Find what you're missing here."
For so long . . .

Little did I realize that "so long"
       eventually becomes "longing."
The notes begin to blur on the page;
       the symphony becomes a solo;
       the voice becomes hoarse and strained.

The music becomes difficult to play;
       the notes no longer make sense;
       the melody is conflicted, uncertain, dissonant, faint.

Without all the other voices—
>   without the blanket of background noise,
>   I finally hear exposed what must have been there all along:
>   A still, small voice gently singing:
>>   "Lost and Found!
>>   Find what you're missing here!"

It is a voice that invites me to learn a new melody.
It is a voice that teaches me rich, vibrant harmonies.
It is a voice that helps me to hear beauty
>   even in the dissonance.

It fills my song with grace notes,
>   adding color and timbre to my melody.
It invites me to join in a wondrous chorus—
>   never to sing alone—never alone.
It sings with me as I sing my song,
>   and sings for me when I scarcely have breathe to sing.

"Lost and Found!
>   Find what you're missing here!"

Lost and Found!
>   How sweet the sound!

I once was lost but now am found.
>   Was deaf, but now I hear,
>   Was blind, but now I see!

Amazing grace indeed!

*The Stone**

Cold, dark rock,
    immovable—
        casting its shadow over the garden,
        entombing life within its silent, dark chambers.

We know only too well
    those stones that weigh heavy on our hearts—
        grief, death, illness,
        loneliness, sin, shame, guilt,
        addiction, depression, broken relationships—
    the landscape of our lives
        is littered with these rocks,
            boulders that block our path
                and keep us from life.

Like the women that first Easter morning,
    we wonder,
        "Who will roll away the stone?"

It is too big,
    too imposing for our limited strength alone to move.
Our energy and thoughts become consumed by its presence,
    and we lose the purpose of our journey.
It becomes the stone around our neck that drowns us,
    suffocating life and hope.

But when we finally arrive at the place of the stone,
    we discover that the stone has been rolled back—
    not removed, but moved just enough
        to allow the power of the resurrected Christ
            to be set free in the world.

God has the power to roll the stone away.

In God's hands,
> the stone entraping us and sealing out life
>> can become the foundation for new life.

In God's hands,
> the boulder causing us to stumble
>> can become the pavement for a new path.

In God's hands,
> the rock casting its shadow over us
>> can be refined and polished
> to become a beautiful gem
>> reflecting the light of God's love and power
>>> to all who see it.

Christ is risen!
> Christ is risen indeed!

God has rolled away the stone;
> life, love, grace, power, light
>> break forth into the darkness of our lives.
And life will never be the same.

*This poem first appeared in the Sept./Oct. 2000 issue of *ALIVE NOW* magazine published by The Upper Room.

A Prayer to a Listening God
Reflections on Exodus

Part I: Thesis

The Listener's head turns,
>ear cupped in the palm of the hand,
>body straining to decipher the garbled sounds heard.

"Say it again; you don't always speak so clearly.
Please, I promise I will understand;
>please, say it again."

The Listener leans forward,
>stretching and extending,
>trying every angle possible to hear the words.

Finally, leaving the place of dwelling
>and moving ever closer,
>the Listener becomes as one
>>with those crying to be heard and understood.

Entering into their world,
>extending across and beyond boundaries,
>>the Listener graciously says,

"I will be who I will be;
>and all of my being leads me here to you.
I am here with you;
>I haven't forgotten you.
I've come just for you,
>and I will do whatever it takes
>>for you to know my love.

Let me hear what you have to say.
I will speak your language;
       speak to me.
            I will listen.
            I will understand; for you are mine."

Part II: Antithesis

They leaned against the wall in the bright, scorching sun—
        weary, too weary to speak . . .
     nomadic wanderers in this strange land
          of cities and buildings made of stone.

Their body language spoke words
   that their voices were too weak to say,
   loud shouts in the soundless silence.

Legs bowed as if the body's weight was too much to bear . . .
        Head bowed down . . .
        Eyes riveted to the ground . . .
        Back bent over as if carrying a heavy burden . . .
           . . . all spoke of a nameless bondage,
          a loss of dignity,
          a tomb that seemed to shut out
              any hope for deliverance.

They yearned for a home—
        a place to call their own.

It was every person's dream—
        a promise spoken by their fathers and mothers,
           their grandparents and ancestors before them.

(continued)

"Someday," the saints of old would sing as a comforting lullaby,
    "Someday, you'll have what we can only dream.
        Someday, the dream will come true for you."

But the dream seemed a cruel mirage
    in the hot afternoon sun.

And someday never seemed to come.

Day built upon day . . .
Time followed after time . . .
    seconds felt like decades,
    moments like the passing of generations.

And with each passing moment,
    another hope died—
        yet another victim to the oppression.

The laborers did what they had to do to survive,
    Working in stony silence—
    Together, yet painfully alone.
Each forced movement added another layer
    to the wall of separation . . .
    brick upon brick
    pain upon pain.

Doesn't Anyone hear their plight?
Doesn't Anyone care?

Can anyone believe the promises
    that Anyone says anymore?

Until, after what felt like years
> of silence and bondage endured,
>> a word was heard.

The sound was but a whisper,
> spoken as if someone else were speaking for them,
> giving voice to the pain felt and the hope lost.

Part III: Synthesis

And God said,
"I have turned my face to my people,
> and I have heard their cries.

I have seen their affliction,
> and I will deliver them as on eagle's wings
>> to a promised place—
>> to a land flowing with milk and honey."

O God, our bondages are many;
> and our energy is too often spent building walls
>> that separate us from one another and from you.

We confess that we are in bondage to sin
> and cannot free ourselves;
yet we so often act as though we can.

In our stumbling attempts to break free,
> we find ourselves sinking ever deeper into the muddy mire;
> and the burdens overwhelm us.

We labor in the heat of the day,
> and so often the labor feels hopeless,
>> unproductive, useless against the forces that oppress us.

(continued)

The weight of our bondage becomes so heavy
   that even our voices—our pleas—
      become silence . . .
        a deep, lonely, God-forsaken silence,
   and we wonder if anyone—if you—
     even care.

And yet, as with the people of old,
   you hear our silent cries.

You give us one another
   to speak that which we in our pain cannot speak.

You give us your Word
   that utters those things we cannot find the words to say.

And not only do you give us the words to speak,
   but you also turn your ear to us and hear us,
     even when all we have strength to whisper is,
      "Lord, in your mercy,
       Hear our prayer."

For you have promised to hear us.

You have promised
   to turn your face to shine upon us.
You have promised to lead us
   to new places along our journey.
You have promised to be our shade
   when the heat of the day saps our strength
     and the well of hope runs dry.

And you have promised, even in the silence,
   to give us the sweet sound of peace.

Home

Cars fly by, propelled in haste
    to make the deadline, win the race.

Days fly by without a trace
    of cooling wind or sacred space
        for solitude, or time to taste
            the banquet of simplicity.

Lives fly by—a blur of face
    and age and need and speech and race—
All clamoring to state their case,
    to claim our time, to set our pace.
        They fill us with perplexity.

Yet in this world of haste and race,
    of days we waste
    and lives misplaced,
Through God's great love we find a place
    of light and space,
    of flow'r-filled vase

Where wandering, harried lives embrace
    quietness, peace, forgiveness, grace . . .
Where stains of sin are washed, erased,
    and hospitality makes the profane chaste . . .
        a place we can call "Home."

The Pearl

Buried under fathoms of murky-laden sea
Lay a shell of someone I used to know as "Me."

Waters splashing, always churning—
Will the tremors ever stop?
Will the shaking ever cease?
Will the current make me drop
     Precious cargo, gifts long-gathered,
     Dross-burned treasures, gold refined,
     Skills honed sharply, polished rhetoric,
     Traits I simply thought as "Mine?"

Will these steps join stuttered words
Shuffling, stammering to be free
From this rusty, clamp-closed prison,
From this place I fear I'll be?

Distant, ever more self-conscious,
I retreat into my shell.
Bailing water—laborious effort—
All seems hopeless . . . But then there fell

Into those dark and murky waters
A grain of windswept sand
Pure as crystal, bright as morning,
Memory of forgotten land.

Within my shell, the grain did enter;
Lodging deep within my flesh
Inducing forth both pain and pleasure,
Joy and sorrow, lives did mesh.

Bound together, strength from struggle,
Beauty borne in storm-tossed sea
Comes the pearl of priceless treasure:
The gift of "Us"—the gift of "Me."

The Lone Oak Tree

A lone oak tree once stood
    in a meadow at my parents' farm.

Its trunk was broad and gnarled,
    telling its history in its rings and blemishes;
its twisted branches bearing witness to the passing of seasons:
    the drought of '59
    the hurricane winds of '68
    the unexpected freeze of '90.

Its graceful canopy, bending down to touch the ground,
    enveloped the grass beneath it
        like a mother holding her newborn child,
        cradled and protected in her strong, gentle arms.

Many a day, the tree held me—
    its strength my consolation and refuge.

It was under her branches that tears were shed,
    prayers were offered,
    questions asked,
    secrets shared with whatever of nature's ears were there to hear.

And nature listened
    in the soft evening winds, which cooled the summer heat . . .
    in the wet morning dew, which soaked my canvas-clad feet . . .
    in the lullaby sung in duet by mother cow and her baby calf . . .
        nature heard and gave response.

It had been years since I had visited that tree.

I, too, knew the passing of seasons.
Rings and blemishes and twisted limbs bore witness
    to the storms and struggles of life.
Tossed by the wilderness winds
    blowing from all directions,
I returned to that meadow
    to find refuge and strength once more
        in the shade of that lone oak tree.

But it had been forced to endure one too many storms.

A violent wind, a crashing bolt had split the tree—
    its shelter shattered into fragments
    its bark stripped
    its canopy ripped open to the scorching sun.
Now I stood in the meadow alone.

And the place that was a refuge
    now felt dangerous, unfamiliar, exposed.

No longer could I hide beneath protective leaves;
No longer could I wrap myself within its embrace.

Alone now,
    nature's response was filled with sounds
    frightening and unwelcomed—
the haunting cry of the coyote pack,
    tormenting me with its monotone song,
    the verse individualized, the refrain always the same . . .
the buzzing sound of a stinging bee . . .
the rattle of the snakes of venom,
    warning of their intent to strike.

(continued)

I stood alone, grieving the loss of this place of peace and rest.
No longer did nature feel safe;
   no longer did nature seem to hear.

With body bent from the burden of cares,
   and head bowed down to leave,
   eyes fixed on the ground,
I looked and saw a lone acorn,
   partially buried under the brush and the fallen branches.

An acorn—sole fruit of this lone oak tree.

And in the distance,
   I heard the furious flutter of quail—
   food from heaven for the weary wilderness wanderers of old.

I picked up the seed of the tree,
   and I carried it with me across that great, vast, frightening meadow.

That acorn is still with me, even with me now,
   as I patiently, sometimes fearfully, wait and work
      for the time and place to plant it in fertile ground,
      where once again a lush meadow will flourish,
         and a lone tree will grow strong and vibrant,
            lasting until the end of my days.

Lingering
(Emmanuel—God with us)

As the fragrance of wild flowers intertwine,
Or the scent of robust, rich vintage wine
Wafts unseen, silent, a mystery—
So your Presence lingers inside of me.

As incense rises a word of prayer
Heaven-bent, unspoken, yet still it is there;
As hearts bound together are somehow set free—
E'en so your Presence lingers inside of me.

Beyond time, beyond place, Beyond logical thought,
Beyond reason and season, Beyond "surely" and "ought,"
Beyond sorrow and doubt, Beyond what eyes can see—
Still your Presence lingers inside of me.

Listening to your melodies

- In what ways is God with us in times of illness and loss?
- Why is it difficult at times to sense God's presence?
- What have you found helpful in those times?
- How has your awareness of God's presence in your life changed over time?
- Where is a place you call "home?"

4

Accompaniment

A vocal or instrumental part that supports another, often solo, part

Our soul waits for the Lord; he is our help and shield. Our heart is glad in him, because we trust in his holy name.

   ↦ *Psalm 33:20-21*

The Lord said to Moses, "What of your brother Aaron, the Levite? I know that he can speak fluently; even now he is coming out to meet you, and when he sees you his heart will be glad. He indeed shall speak for you to the people; he shall serve as a mouth for you."

   ↦ *Exodus 4:14,16*

A Christian community is a healing community not because wounds are cured and pains are alleviated, but because wounds and pains become openings or occasions for a new vision. Mutual confession then becomes a mutual deepening of hope, and sharing weakness becomes a reminder to one and all of the coming strength.

   ↦ *Henri J. M. Nouwen*

Henri J. M. Nouwen, *The Wounded Healer*, Image Books, a division of Doubleday & Company, Inc., 1979, p. 94.

The melody of my life

Along the journey of illness and loss, I have been sustained by the love and care of others. I have been blessed with loving and supportive people as well as caring communities of faith. They have walked the journey of illness and loss with me, and have given of themselves in countless ways. Their support has been a true blessing.

But in a paradoxical way, the need of their support has also been a source of frustration. The need to rely more and more on the care of others has meant that the illness is progressing. There are days when feelings of inadequacy and dependency color the melody of my relationships with others. I even find myself frustrated with the language used—"disability"—seeming to imply someone less than whole.

I have learned it is important for me to feel I have something to offer in my relationships with others—I can still offer care to those who care for me.

The Face of God

I give you a new commandment, that you love one another. Just as I have loved you . . .
> *John 13:34*

Who can define what love is?

How can one describe
>the feel of the wind to someone who has no sense of touch?
Can the blue of the sky
>be fully seen by those who have no sight?

Who can define God?

Transcendent, paradoxical,
>always near, yet always beyond the reach
>>of our imagination . . .
>always present, yet never seen . . .

Now we see in a mirror dimly;
>but then—then we shall see face-to-face . . .

Then becomes now . . .
>Realized eschatology.
In the Beloved, God and love intersect;
>Emmanuel—God with us;
>Fusion—horizontal and vertical are no more,
>>Future is melded to present,
>>Promise becomes fulfillment.
>>Human and Divine join as one.

For to love someone
>is to see the face of God.

I May Be

I may be ill,
> but Your love for me still stands healthy and strong.

I may be stumbling,
> but Your love for me still guides my footsteps
>> and causes my feet to skip.

I may be weak,
> but Your love for me still has the power to move mountains
>> and overcome all that stands against us.

I may be sad,
> but Your love for me still shines in the gloom of the night.

I may be weeping,
> but Your love for me still brings laughter
>> and a lively dance to my heavy soul.

I may be in pain,
> but Your love for me is still a healing balm,
>> which calms the broken, scarred heart.

I may be trembling,
> but Your love for me still stands as a solid rock,
>> firmly laid in the foundations of the earth.

I may be grieving and know death,
> but Your love for me still brings life and
>> blessed resurrection.

I may be,
> but through Your love for me,
>> I now can become.

I Am Here
(Bear one another's burdens)

I hear it in your voice—
>	faint, but a whisper,
>	any other volume requiring too much . . . too much . . .

I feel it in your tears—
>	silent drops from a soul saturated with sorrow.

I feel it in your words—
>	absent, unspoken, spent.

And I write these brief lines
>	as strings around a finger to remind you—
>		I Am Here.

Though this voice be halting,
>	weakened by growing illness,
>	it is strong enough to speak in intercession
>		to the very throne of God for you.

Though these arms be trembling,
>	quivering in the damp dew of disability,
>	they are strong enough to hold you
>		secure and still.

Though these legs be faltering,
>	stumbling over obstacles unforeseen,
>	they are strong enough to walk
>		steady and sure beside you.

Though this soul be grieving,
>>weary from journeys through valleys and shadows,
>>it is strong enough to carry your sorrow
>>>strong and willingly for you.

Don't you see:
>>I Am Here.

No longer do you have to be
>>the lone voice in the silent din of need . . .
No longer do you have to be
>>the only steady arm amidst the tumultuous world . . .
No longer do you have to be
>>the only steps that dare not falter . . .
>>the only tears that dare not fall . . .
>>the only soul that dares not sorrow . . .
>>>For I Am Here.

Travel no more the journey alone;
>>For I Am Here.
>>>I am Here.
>>>I am hear.
>>>I am here.

As an Ancient Woman

(Love) bears all things, believes all things, hopes all things, endures all things.

    ℗ *1 Corinthians 13:7*

Like an ancient woman,
       who walks miles in the heat of the day
              to bring life-giving water to the ones she loves,
You continue to walk this long, pain-filled journey with me.

The elements you bear
       sustain my life,
       wash away the dirt on my soiled existence,
       and gently cleanse my wounds.

You could have chosen another path.
       You could have waited at the end of the road
           for me to arrive there by myself.
       You could have let someone else carry the load.
You could have let me carry it alone.

But no,
       You choose to express your love,
           not so much in words, as I have often done
              (for words are easy to write).
       You choose to express your love in deeds,
           a reflection of a depth of love
              that words cannot capture or contain.

You choose to walk the Christ-like path,
       who, when asked the measure of love for another,
       stretched out strong arms
           and bore the suffering and pain of the other.

You walk this path freely—
>   with little thought to the wounds you yourself bear—
>>   for me—all for me.

Today, put down that burden and rest.

Today, let me care for you.

Let me walk the dusty road for you.
Let me wash your wounds,
>   and kiss your feet,
>   and bandage your cracked, bruised heels.

Let me care for you as you have cared for me.

Today, hear my prayer of thanksgiving to God for you.

For God has come to me
>   in the tired body of an ancient woman
>>   whose love is so great
>>>   she bears this heavy, pain-filled load
>>>>   for me . . . all for me.

Tapestry

What an incredible design
     God weaves in our common life together—
        the blue of Advent hope,
        the white and gold of festivals of life
            (Easter, Christmas, baptisms, all saints),
        the royal purple of passion and suffering,
        the red of the flames of the Spirit,
           inspiring and re-forming us,
        the green of spiritual growth.

God takes these colors of our shared life
        and creates a beautiful mosaic of memories—
          a sacred, beautiful tapestry.

The colors at times blend together in our mind's eye;
     but some stand out boldly—
        joys and sorrows,
        life and death,
        pain and peace,
          all interwoven in the fabric of life.

There are places in the tapestry
     that are frayed and worn—
        reminders that our life together
        has its moments of challenge and struggle.

There are times
     when the threads of patience and care
     are worn thin,
        when we do not love as we ought.

But sown around those threadbare moments
>are the strong cords of God's forgiveness and grace,
>>allowing the pattern to take shape again,
>>>all the more beautiful,
>>>all the more interwoven
>>>>and interconnected.

The tapestry God creates through our life together
>is filled with a variety of textures—
>>each one unique,
>>each one adding to the strength and beauty
>>of the fabric.

God weaves us together,
>patiently sewing a beautiful design.

Our lives are bound together;
>and even as others come and bring their own unique texture
>>and color to the weave,
>the Weaver is able to take who and what we are
>>and pattern in the loom of the church
>>>a tapestry for all to see—
>>>a witness to the grace and love of God.

No matter where we go,
>the patterns of our lives will reflect this tapestry
>that God's guiding hand makes.

And our lives are all the richer and more beautiful
>because of the tapestry of which we are a part.

The Cup
(For the care giver)

Alone I sit in the crowded room—
> hands shaking across the page,
> arms quivering with no relief of electronic pulse
>> or medicinal aid allowed.

The shaking gets progressively worse and worse as I wait.

And I wish she were here,
> not so much for my sake as much as for hers.

For I wonder,
> "Does she know what is being asked?"

She hasn't seen the full effects of this frustrating illness—
> the hand that won't rest or remain still,
> the legs that won't quite move,
> the muscles that remain taut and tight.

With each passing minute,
> the hands shake a bit more,
> the legs stiffen,
>> and I wonder:
>>> "Does she really know what is before us?
>>> Does she know what is being asked?"

Alone I sit in the crowded room—
> surrounded by the aged in wheelchairs
>> and leaning on canes,
> unable to move on their own,
> depending on loved ones to help with basic bodily needs.

Alone I sit—
 stiff and yet shaking, all at once,
 not knowing what is before me,
  yet wanting to know . . .
 ready to live,
  yet fearing what kind of life it will be . . .
 wanting her support with me in the years to come,
  yet fearful of the demands that the years may bring.

Dare I ask her to bear such a burden?
Does she really know what could be before us?

I want her here,
 not for my solace,
  but so that she knows—fully knows—
 and in knowing, can honestly and realistically
  answer the call
 and realize the cup that is before me
  I have little choice but to drink.

Listening to your melodies

- Who has God given you to walk with on your journey?
- In what ways has does your community (church, support group, friends) offer support to others in times of illness and loss?
- How would you advise your community respond to those who have no one to accompany them in times of need?
- Have you experienced times when you felt dependent upon others? How did you respond? Were you able to feel as though you had something to offer others as well?
- When an illness or loss occurs, how can you be a support and accompaniment for others ?

5

Grace Notes

Ornamentations used to decorate or embellish a melody

O give thanks to the Lord, for (the Lord) is good, for his steadfast love endures forever.

∵ *Psalm 136: 1*

And slowly I learned. I learned what I must have forgotten somewhere in my busy, well-planned, and very "useful" life. I learned that everything that is, is freely given by the God of love. All is grace. Light and water, shelter and food, work and free time, children, parents and grandparents, birth and death—it is all given to us. Why? So that we can say **gracias**, *thanks: thanks to God, thanks to each other, thanks to all and everyone.*

∵ *Henri J. M. Nouwen*

Henri J. M. Nouwen, *Gracias: A Latin American Journal*, Harper and Row, 1983, p. 187.

The melody of my life

Throughout the years of living with Parkinson's disease, I have heard countless unexpected melodies in my life's song. Some have been joyous and hope-filled—new relationships, new medications and surgical procedures that have brought stability and restored functioning. Others have been somber and pain-filled—broken relationships, disappointing results of tests, procedures, medications.

Like many who experience chronic illness, I rely on medication to cope with its symptoms and to gain some measure of relief. While I am thankful for the wonderful therapeutic power of medication, I also know the frustration of having the day measured by the scheduled dosages.

These ups and down—full of joys and sadness, melodies and silences—have been the "grace notes" of my life—moments that have added color, depth, and richness to the music. Through these notes, I have learned much about illness, health, life, death, happiness, sorrow—and about myself.

The Curse and the Blessing

Now, I know.

For these many years,
   I have always answered the question
      by pointing to the hidden blessing.
"Perhaps God has used the Parkinson's,"
   I say courageously,
      "to enhance my ministry.
As I share my weakness and my struggle,
   I allow others to share their struggle.
   I give voice and words to the grief."

It was the best—the only—answer I could with any integrity give
   to this unexplained suffering and affliction,
      this thorn of the flesh.

At times, I want to curse the All-Powerful God
   who allows illness, sorrow, and loss to exist.

But then I see the cross;
   and I begin to truly see.

Upon this thorn
   has come a beautiful rose—
      a rich, fragrant flower painted in word and verse.

I realize now
>> that this rose would not have come to bud
>>> save for the thorn;
>> and the beauty and glory of this precious flower
>>> could have not blossomed
>>>> were it not for the watering of the tears
>>>> from the pain of the suffering and affliction.

And once more,
>> the cross becomes the crown
>> the thorn becomes the flower
>> and the curse becomes the blessing
>>> in the powerful, creative hands of God.

Hymn to the Apothecary

In the morning when I rise . . .
>> The rhythm and rhyme
>>> of Morning Prayer and Compline
>> Now augmented
>>> with potents invented
>>>> to chase the demon away.

I need thee, O I need thee,
>> every hour I need thee . . .
>> I cannot go an hour,
>>> without their medicinal power,
>>> my constant companions on this uncharted way.

Count your blessings,
>> name them one by one . . .
>> Every morning the same ritual,
>>> regimented, habitual:
>> Seven at daybreak, two at night,
>>> four at the noontime, four at twilight—
>>>> each its own rubric, instruction, and say.

Red and yellow, black and white,
>> they are precious in the sight . . .
>> A rainbow of color, of size and of shape:
>>> red, white, and yellow. Tablet, capsule I take
>>>> to begin and end the day.

I know my own,
>> my own know me . . .
>> I know them so well,
>> By their sounds I can tell
>>> their identity as I stir them
>>>> in the bottles where they lay.

Without your grace, we waste away
>> Like flowers that whither and decay . . .
>> As the illness evolves
>>> more and more, life revolves
>>>> around their powers to keep pain at bay.

Bane and blessing,
>> pain and pleasure . . .
>> 'Tis the odd, strange contradiction:
>>> The very means of addiction
>>>> have become my companion, my strength, my stay.

The Dance

Slowly, I learn—
>   I, the straight-A student.

Slowly I learn this hard lesson of living:

The color of love is seen
>   only as joy and pain join together in the same dance.

To enjoy the full exhilaration of the dance,
>   one must be willing to learn new steps,
>   to come to know the movements and needs
>   of the partner.

One must be willing to lead and to follow,
>   to give and to receive,
>   to trust and to be entrusted.

There are awesome movements in life's dance that give great joy—
>   times when grace and selfless love are joined together,
>   times when the steps are in synch with the music
>   and the two are one.

And there are movements in the dance
>   when the steps falter,
>   when the motion is halting, uncertain,
>   when toes are stepped on,
>   and the music is faint,
>   and fear and pain are felt.

But the full colors of the dance are known
>   only as both joy and pain are joined.

For love is not a dim, light red hue,
      but deep, blood-red crimson,
a beautiful color known only
      as the dark colors of pain
      are joined with the bright colors of joy.

Sophia–Wisdom
(A reflection on Ecclesiastes 1)

"Would you like to dance?" she asked,
> a playful lilt in her voice.
>> "You only go around once,
>>> and life is so full of wonder."

The music of the dance began,
> its rhythm at times gentle and soothing,
>> full of contentment and delight,
> at other times ominous and dark,
>> foreboding with sorrow and futile toil.

I came to know her
> through the varied songs that night.

Her name was Sophia,
> wise beyond her years.
She had known much in life;
> and as we swayed together to the music,
>> she gracefully moved from one subject to the next:

"You know," she began,
> "I believe there's a time and place for everything—
>> a time for laughing,
>> and a time for crying;
>> a time to be quiet,
>> and a time to sing so loud
>>> even the deaf sit up and take notice."

Her eyes sparkled
> as she whirled around and laughed out loud.

As she spun back toward me,
>   she glanced at the other couples on the dance floor.

"Isn't it a shame
>   that we spend so much time trying to find happiness,
>   when in the end,
>   it is happiness that really finds us?"

"What do you mean?" I asked.

"Well, just look at all those folk," she said,
>   spinning me around so that I faced the crowd as we danced.
"They're working so hard—
>   so full of themselves.
And for what?
For a few fleeting moments of feeling good.

And yet, when the sun comes up tomorrow,
>   will any of it make any difference?"

She was quiet for a moment.
She stopped dancing,
>   a far away look of reflective contemplation
>   taking her to places unknown.

"No, sir," she said softly.
"I'll tell you where to look
>   if you want to find true happiness.
The beauty of true love—
>   that's where happiness is.
A life well-lived—
>   that's a treasure beyond measure.
Being true to yourself—
>   you'll find what you're looking for.

(continued)

Knowing who and whose you are—
>> and by God you'll have the greatest gift of all."

Her voice became a whisper
>> as she paused again:
"But you know,
>> you really can't find any of these things on your own.
In the end, if you're lucky,
>> they find you."

She stood still as a wise, old oak.
And then she flashed a big smile that lit up the room,
>> twirled around twice to the beat of the music,
>> and with a sparkle in her eyes she said,

"But we sure can do a lot of foolish things
>> that get in the way of them finding us!"

With that exclamation,
>> she laughed with sheer delight,
>> and gracefully glided off the dance floor,
>> leaving me entranced to reflect
>> on my rich encounter with Sophia,
>> the embodiment of Wisdom.

Listening to your melodies

- What "grace notes" have decorated and embellished your life?
- What have been some of the joys and promising events you've experienced in your own journey?
- What have been some of the disappointments and setbacks?
- What have you learned along the way?

6

Reprise

A return to an original theme

Sing to the Lord, bless his name; tell of his salvation from day to day.

❧ *Psalm 96: 2*

We cannot live our lives constantly looking back, listening back, lest we be turned to pillars of longing and regret, but to live without listening at all is to live deaf to the fullness of the music. Sometimes we avoid listening for fear of what we may hear, sometimes for fear that we may hear nothing at all but the empty rattle of our own feet on the pavement. But . . . "Be not afraid," says another, "for lo, I am with you always, even unto the end of the world." He says he is with us on our journeys. He says he has been with us since each of our journeys began. Listen for him. Listen to the sweet and bitter airs of your present and your past for the sounds of him.

❧ *Frederich Buechner*

Frederick Buechner, *The Sacred Journey,* Harper & Row, 1982, pp. 77-78.

The melody of my life

The movements continue in my life, full of harmonies and dissonance. I still wrestle with the challenges and struggles of a chronic illness. I still am acutely aware of its implications for my life, my work, and my relationships with others. I still have days where I grieve the losses the illness has brought.

At times, I feel like a passive recipient—I have no choice but to take what the illness brings. And to a certain extent, that's true. But I have come to realize that I do have choices in the matter. I can choose to live life fully within the limitations I have. I can choose to savor each day as a gift from God and see the many ways I have been blessed because of and in spite of this affliction. I can choose to be open to see how God will use my brokenness to bring about wholeness, how God will use my illness to bring about healing.

And I can choose to keep listening for the melodies of grace . . . and to try to keep singing.

Choose Life

*Only be strong and very courageous, being careful to act in accordance
with all the law that my servant Moses commanded you; do not turn
from it to the right hand or to the left, so that you may be successful
wherever you go.*

    Joshua 1:6-7

*Choose this day whom you will serve . . . as for me and my household,
we will serve the Lord.*

    Joshua 24:15

Eenie, meenie, minie, mo . . .

       She loves me, she loves me not . . .
       Heads, you win; tails, you lose . . .
       Just close your eyes and pick one . . .
       Pull a name out of the hat . . .
       Spin the bottle . . .

Some choices are so simple and made so arbitrarily
       we seldom give them another thought.

And some are so painful and life-changing
       we lie awake at night agonizing over the decision
           long before and long after it is made.

Is that how our decision is for you, O God?

In many ways,
       the decision is so simple and obvious
          we don't need to ponder it.

(continued)

CHOOSE LIFE!
>>Follow the One who has brought us through the wilderness
>>>and led us dry-shod through the raging sea,
>>who has guided us to a promised land of peace and joy.
How could we choose otherwise?

And yet,
your promised place in our life is not so easily claimed.

We look ahead and see giants dwelling there.

Obstacles stand before us at every turn,
>>seeking to claim our allegiance,
>>fighting for their place,
>>causing us to retreat.

In the crucible of clashing choices,
>>we become scattered and divided into various camps;
>>we lose sight of the promise.
Like the ark of the covenant for the people of Israel,
>>that which is central to who and what we are
>>is captured by our enemy and taken away.

And we begin to see that choosing life
>is no arbitrary or simple decision.

Choosing life means standing up
>>against all the forces that deny life,
>>all the giants that taunt us and claim ownership
>>>to the promises that we thought were ours.

Choosing life means confronting
>>those places in our lives that bring death and separation,
>>>division and sorrow.

The weapons we have in the confrontation
>seem to be so inadequate—
>>a slingshot against Goliath,
>>an army equipped with trumpets
>>>to overthrow the walls of Jericho.

But you, O God,
>give us one other weapon.
You give us your Word,
>which had the power to create the world
>>and turn darkness into light
>>and chaos into order.
You give us your Word,
>which commanded the roaring seas to be still.
You give us your Word,
>which became flesh and overcame the power of death and sin.
You give us your Word,
>which promises to be with us always, even to the end of the age.
You give us your Word . . .

In our struggle of competing choices, O God,
>remind us again of the promise and power of your Word.
Give us strength and courage
>to dare to choose life.
Set our minds and hearts toward you alone,
>that we might know the inexpressible joys
>>of life in you.

The Journey

When the days drew near for (Jesus) to be taken up, he set his face to go to Jerusalem.

  ✨ *Luke 9:51*

How many more steps are there?
How many more blind curves do I have to travel?
Does the road ever come to an end?

I know the end of the story;
  I have seen a glimpse of what resurrection life can be.
Light has shined in the dark caverns of lifeless years.

But between me and the Easter light where I long to be
  is a path filled with dangerous terrain:
   rocks, unexpected detours, forks that call forth decisions.

There are well-meaning guides along the way
  who know a certain path,
  but can't even begin to imagine taking a different road.

At times along the journey
  I can see clearly the destination,
   and I am inspired to remain steadfast.

But there are times
  when the way is so difficult, the terrain so treacherous
   that it takes all my energy and concentration
    to just keep going.

How long, O Lord, how long?
How much farther do I have to walk?
Isn't there some other way?

From Silence to Song

Part 1: The Silence—"What If's"

I think they're afraid of the light.

While the sun still sends its silk-threaded stream of radiance
    weaving in and out, up and down,
      over and under the patchwork earth of water and soil,
    they remain hidden, unseen, gone.

But when the eyes close the curtain on the drama of the day,
    and the lights fade on the final scene,
from the shadows they come—
    a silent, invisible, dark force invading peaceful rest.

"What if's" . . .

What if the illness progresses rapidly?
What if I can no longer
    remember words to write?
What if I tremble with such a frantic, fevered pitch
    that I will not be able to be who and how I hope to be?
What if . . .

The dark unknown of the future
    is too frightening to contemplate,
      too full of them.

So I turn; and frantic, run to the past,
    only to discover their rising in memory's shadows as well.

(continued)

What if . . .
What if I had done something else?
What if I had said a different word,
      or given another day,
      or seen a different view?
What if . . .

The future fills with anxiety;
      the past—with guilt and regret.

Frantically, fearfully,
      burden-filled, I run to the "now."

Part 2: The Song

Now, I am.
Here, I stand—
      bombarded on all sides by silent sounds, loud and shrill:
           "What if" . . . Screams the past.
           "What if" . . . Shouts the future.
              "What if . . . what if"

The din of their silent voices almost drowns one other sound—
      a whisper,
           soft, yet sure,
           faint, yet clear . . .
      a whisper:
           "The light shines in the darkness,
              and the darkness has not overcome it."

The light shines . . .
Slowly dawn's first rays begin to break through the dark night,
            and I hear, as if the first morning,
                        its subtle, present sound.
The light *shines* . . .
        Not "shined,"
                bound and imprisoned
                        in a forever-changeless, unforgiving past
        Not "will shine,"
                bouncing aimlessly
                        in a forever-changing future

But "SHINES"
        Here, now, in this dark night of "what if's"
"SHINES"
        In this present hour
"SHINES"
        In her . . . in him . . . in me
"SHINES" . . .

"The light shines in the darkness,
        and the darkness has not overcome it."

The voice is gradually more clearly heard—
            a swelling chorus, singing of the present:
        "Your sins *are* forgiven."
        "The kingdom of God *is* at hand."
        "*Today* you shall be with me in paradise."
        "*Now* the Spirit's invitation; *now* the Son's epiphany.
                        Now . . . now . . . now."

(continued)

"What if's" still cast their silent shadows;
       guilt and regret, fear and anxiety
             still linger in the dark memory of past
                  and the dim vision of future.

But this day—
       this day I am gifted with the present:
            "The Light shines in the darkness,
                and the darkness has not overcome it."

Grant courage, O Lord, to savor the day.
Grant courage, O Lord, to sing your praise.
Grant courage, O Lord, and teach us to pray:
          "Give us this day . . ."
             Amen; give us this day.

Listening to your melodies

- What choices do you have when dealing with illness and loss?
- Why is it so difficult to see options at times? Are there times when there really are no options?
- What becomes important when facing illness and loss?
- What melody do you hear as you "listen to your life?"

Program Notes

Insights on the musical movements written in prose

Make me to know your ways, O Lord; teach me your paths. Lead me in your truth, and teach me.

    ⟨⟩ *Psalm 25:4-5*

When I attend a concert, I find it helpful to have program notes that elaborate and offer insight about the musical composition. The notes which follow are samplings of newsletter articles ("program notes") written in prose to add insight to the composition of my life.

                                                             JMB

∞

For "The Cantus Firmus": Be Not Afraid

This newsletter article was written a few days before Christmas, and shortly after surgery to implant a stimulator in the thalamus of the brain to treat the tremors associated with Parkinson's disease.

"Be not afraid," the angel said to the young girl named Mary, announcing the incredible news that she was going to be the mother of the Christ child.

"Be not afraid," the angel said to the terrified shepherds on the Judean hillside that first Christmas night.

"Be not afraid."

This has been a strange Advent season for me. Being away from my pastoral duties because of the surgery and recovery has made this season feel disjointed and a bit uncertain. Many of the Advent themes—hope, anticipation, expectation, preparation—have been all too real for me in a completely different way this year. There was the preparation for being away and the preparation for the surgery. There was great expectation of the longed-for results of the procedure, followed by frustration and disappointment, and then renewed hope. There was anticipation of returning to a leadership role in worship; and there was some uncertainty of when I would be strong enough to be back full time.

And, to be honest, there was fear. What if the surgery wasn't successful? What if we weren't able to get the adjustments on the stimulator quite right? What if the side effects continued? What if I'm not strong enough to return to full-time ministry? Those fears—perhaps unspoken until now—were there for me, and perhaps for you, too.

We all, in one way or another, know the feeling of fear. Perhaps it's the fear of getting older and losing strength and health; perhaps it's the fear of an uncertain future in our work. Or maybe it's the fear of losing a loved one, or the fear of what will happen in a relationship that is stretched to near breaking.

The fears are real. But the good news that breaks in upon our fear this and every Christmas season is the word of the angel: "Be not afraid." It is a word that doesn't take away the concern or the cause of fear; rather, it reminds us that we no longer face the fear alone. Emmanuel—God is with us.

I have felt that Presence this year more profoundly than ever before. I recall times in the surgery (for which I had to remain awake) when the words of Scripture and the power of prayer gave me a sense of profound peace. I recall days of frustration when a note or a card or a phone call was just the healing word I needed to hear.

Granted, there are still fears in our lives. But as Christmas comes once again, we will hear the word of the angels spoken anew to us: "Be not afraid; for behold, I bring you good news of great joy which will come to all the people; for to you is born this day in the city of David a Savior, who is Christ the Lord" (Luke 2:10-11, RSV).

And in our fear-filled world, that birth makes all the difference.

For "Accompaniment": With a Lump in My Throat

This newsletter article followed a Maundy Thursday sermon.

Every Sunday, pastor and congregation engage in a fascinating dialog called the sermon. Those who have heard me preach know that my preaching style is one that is very personal. The good news message is one that has to speak to me—me personally, in my life and situation—in order for me to more authentically share it with you, the congregation.

It is an awesome and sometimes scary thing to approach preaching this way. But being willing to "open the window" to my own experiences of faith and doubt—to let you see my joys and struggles—is a part of who I am as pastor and person. I don't know how to do otherwise. I do so, not so that my experiences are held up as an example, but so that, by God's grace, we can together be connected to one another and to the larger story of God's love and grace in the life, death, and resurrection of Jesus Christ.

Approaching preaching, worship leadership, and pastoral ministry this way can sometimes make for strange and powerful moments. I have found that there are certain phrases, words, melodies, and contexts that have such profound meaning for me that when they occur, I am swept with emotions that make it difficult to speak or sing.

Let me give you some examples. I cannot sing the line in the hymn "For All the Saints" that goes "And hearts are brave again and arms are strong" without a welling up of emotions within me. Those words have a whole different meaning to me as I have struggled with the effects of Parkinson's disease and have felt at times anything but brave or strong. And every Easter Sunday, my voice cracks, and a lump rises in my throat when I try to sing that verse of that hymn.

A similar event happened in worship during the sermon on Maundy Thursday. My sermon title was "What Does Love Look Like?" The sermon had three points: love looks like a towel of servanthood as Jesus washes the disciples' feet; love looks like a meal as Jesus offers himself to us in the Lord's Supper; and love looks like arms extended as God embraces death so that we might be embraced by life.

It was the last point that hit me as I tried to "turn a phrase" that was intimately personal. My sermon notes read: "As we see God's arms outstretched on the cross to embrace the world, we see what God's love looks like. God embraces even death, so that even though our arms be weak and trembling, we are enfolded by the strong arms of a God who shows us just what love looks like."

As I got to "even though our arms be weak and trembling," it happened. The power of those words and what they meant to me in my situation overwhelmed me. For a moment, I couldn't go on. I looked out into the congregation and saw many others with tears as well. And I knew that a fourth point needed to be added to my sermon. I had experienced another example of what love looks like: Love looks like a community of faith where struggles are shared and weakness expressed as a reminder of the promised hope and strength of God.

I still get frustrated with myself when these things happen—when the emotions well up and at times overtake me. I still wish I could speak through them and say what I really want to say. But I have come to realize that even if I can't say the words, God is still communicating what perhaps words cannot express. And I'm learning to pay attention to those times when the lump rises in the throat; for I am beginning to discover that in those times of deep emotion, God just might be speaking in a way I had not been able to hear before.

For "Reprise": A Final Song—Venturing Forth by Faith

This article is a revised version of the newsletter sent to the congregation as I announced my resignation as pastor.

Now the Lord said to Abram, "Go from your country and your kindred and your (family's) house to the land I will show you . . . So Abram went . . .

☞ *Genesis 12:1, 4*

By faith Abraham obeyed when he was called to set out for a place that he was to receive as an inheritance; and he set out, not knowing where he was going.

☞ *Hebrews 11:8*

The 11th chapter of Hebrews is one of the most compelling ever written. The author, verse after verse, recalls the faith of the saints of old. Verse after verse, the same chorus is sung: "By faith . . . " By faith Moses did as God called him to do . . . By faith the people of Israel took that first step through the waters of the Red Sea . . . By faith Joshua fought the battle of Jericho, and the walls came a'tumblin' down . . . By faith Abraham obeyed when he was called to set out, not knowing where he was going . . . By faith.

Abraham and Sarah have become my patron saints these days. I have always wondered what that conversation between Abraham and Sarah must have been like the day he heard the Lord's call to pull up stakes and go—without a sure destination or even a road map. I've always envisioned Abraham bending down as he entered the tent and saying, "Well, Sarah, guess what. We're moving." "Where?" "Don't know. But God's got a plan." And so they packed up and went—by faith.

I'm sure we have all, at one time or another, wrestled with difficult decisions regarding the future. I certainly wrestled with and grieved over the decision to apply for disability. Many times I've asked aloud, "Is this the right time? Is this what you want for me, God?" People with whom I've spoken, in their efforts to reassure me of my decision, continually reminded me of the new opportunities that this will afford me. "You will be able to use your limited energies to do the things you do best; and you'll get to choose what those things are." It has taken me awhile to truly hear those words; and some days, I still can't.

But the more I wrestled and prayed, the more I was drawn to this eleventh chapter of Hebrews and to the refrain written verse after verse: "By faith." And I've begun to view the past in a whole different light.

By faith . . . we trust that the Holy Spirit has been working to bring us to this time and place.

By faith . . . I came to serve as pastor, Parkinson's disease and all, knowing full well that the future might hold a day and decision like this.

By faith . . . I was entrusted with your love, your struggles, your joys, your sorrows; and by faith, I've entrusted the same to you. By faith . . . we have laughed together, cried together, planned and played together, faced surgeries together, wrestled with tough decisions together, and shared life together.

By faith . . . we have gathered around God's word, font, and table where we graciously accept one another's strengths as well as limitations and struggles. And in a very real way, you have empowered me to be able to see strength in my weaknesses.

By faith . . . you have dared to walk a sacred journey with me as we have discovered together the power and presence of God in the midst of a chronic illness and an even more chronic healing and grace.

I would like to think that when Abraham pulled up the last stake holding his tent, and filled the last waterskin for the last time in the familiar watering hole, there must have been a tear in his eye. He was leaving a place that was familiar . . . a people he dearly loved . . . a setting and a way of life that was comfortable and known.

I would also like to think that Abraham, on his journey to places unknown, might have, in his humanness, even asked himself, "Am I absolutely, completely sure that this is what God wants me to do? Is this really what God had in mind?"

The Scriptures don't really tell us if he and Sarah asked these questions (although we do have hints that they did question God about becoming pregnant at an old age). What the Bible does tell us is this: They ventured forth by faith.

Do I grieve the losses implicit with this illness and the choices it has forced me to make? Absolutely.

Will I experience times when I will look back and wonder whether I'm doing the right thing at the right time? Without a doubt.

But like Abraham and Sarah . . . like the saints of old and the saints yet to come . . . I venture forth by faith.

By faith . . . I trust that God has something else in store for me. Maybe it's writing a devotional book for those struggling with chronic illness. Maybe it's being the voice for those whose physical voices have been silenced and whose hands have been stilled by diseases such as Parkinson's. Maybe it's helping a congregation as an interim pastor through the tough transition of facing saying good-bye to a pastor. Maybe it's serving churches struggling with conflicts to help bring healing. Maybe it's teaching . . . or preaching . . . or counseling.

Whatever it will be, I trust by faith that God will be leading and guiding me.

And by faith . . . I trust that God has something wonderful in store for you as well.

Who knows what gifted people God will bring next into your life? Who knows what new and exciting opportunities and ministries are

before you?
Who knows? By faith, we trust that God knows. And so by faith, we venture forth.

And as we go, we pray: "Lord God, you have called your servants to ventures of which we cannot see the ending, by paths as yet untrodden, through perils unknown. Give us faith to go out with good courage, not knowing where we go, but only that your hand is leading us and your love supporting us; through Jesus Christ our Lord." Amen (From Evening Prayer, *Lutheran Book of Worship*, p. 153)

Additional response to *Will I Sing Again?*

John Bade's "mind-stretching, soul-searing, gut-wrenching" work, to borrow a phrase from Robert Shaw, moved me to tears and hope. I will often re-read *Will I Sing Again?* and often recommend it to others before "I shuffle off this mortal coil."

"The Sea of Faith was once full," wrote Matthew Arnold in his melancholy Dover Beach. In contrast "The Sea of Faith is full," for John Bade in his Parkinson's.

Provocative, in-depth, lucid, theological, pastoral, all true. No vapid, feel-good spirituality here. All visceral, like a spirited, Kentucky thoroughbred.

In *Will I Sing Again?* the chronically-ill ministers to the chronically ill and, I predict, to many of us who consider our health a divine right.

Though John Bade is the subject, he names Another as Object. How could it be otherwise? In his Parkinson's John Bade contends the Object is, as in all else, the Center, the crucified and risen Christ.

PAUL W. F. HARMS
Emeritus Professor of Homiletics in Continuing Service
Trinity Lutheran Seminary
Director, Trinity Lutheran Seminary Theatre